Serena Williams

Serena Williams

Michael Bradley

BENCHMARK BOOKS

MARSHALL CAVENDISH
NEW YORK

Benchmark Books
Marshall Cavendish
99 White Plains Road
Tarrytown, NY 10591-9001
www.marshallcavendish.com

Library of Congress Cataloging-in-Publication Data

Bradley, Michael, 1962-
Serena Williams / by Michael Bradley.
v. cm.—(Benchmark all-stars)
Includes bibliographical references and index.
Contents: The Serena slam—The dream begins—First steps—Venus's little sister—
Still searching—On top of the world—Players statistics—Glossary.
ISBN 0-7614-1760-5
1. Williams, Serena, 1981—Juvenile literature. 2. Tennis players—United States—
Biography—Juvenile literature. 3. African American women tennis players—
Biography—Juvenile literature. [1. Williams, Serena, 1981- 2. Tennis players. 3. African
Americans—Biography. 4. Women—Biography.] I. Title II. Series: Bradley, Michael,
1962-   . Benchmark all-stars.

GV994.A2W553 2004
796.342'092--dc22

2003025569

Photo Research by Regina Flanagan

Cover Photograph by Martyn Hayhow/AFP/Corbis.
Simon Bruty/Sports Illustrated: 2–3; AP/Wide World Photos: 6, 9, 10, 12, 18, 22, 24,
26, 28, 33, 34, 35, 36, 39, 40 (top and bottom); Shaun Best/Reuters: 16; Hector
Mata/AFP/Corbis: 27, 32; Matt Campbell/AFP/Corbis: 30; David Gray/Reuters: 41;
Kevin Lamarque/Reuters: 42.

Series design by Becky Terhune
Printed in Italy

1 3 5 6 4 2

Contents

Serena smiles and weeps after defeating her sister in the women's final of the Australian Open Tennis Tournament.

CHAPTER ONE

The Serena Slam

This wasn't like any of the others. Instead of accepting the award at the 2003 Australian Open with her usual blend of confidence and youthful *exuberance*, Serena Williams cried. She did not cry because she had defeated her older sister, Venus, to take the title. She cried because she had become only the fifth woman in the history of women's tennis to hold all four major championships (Australian, French, Wimbledon, and the U.S. Open) at the same time. She cried because she had it all.

Of course, her sobs were tears of joy. The twenty-one-year-old was at the top of the women's tennis game only a year after her career seemed stalled. Sure, Williams had been successful before, but not like this. She had gone from being Venus's little sister to ranking as the best women's tennis player in the world. Some felt that she shouldn't be talking about a "Grand Slam" because she hadn't won all four majors in the same calendar year (she had not won the 2002 Australian Open). Still, no one could argue against her *dominance*. Williams was the best in the world. And her "Serena Slam," as some called her four major wins, was proof of that.

"All of a sudden, a million things came in my head," Williams said after the victory. "I started thinking about all the work I've put into tennis, not just today, not just these two weeks, and not even just the year."

It was a long ride for Serena, one that began when her father, Richard Williams, introduced her to tennis at the age of five. It had included *controversy*, hardship, and plenty of success. After winning in Australia, Williams had captured twenty-two singles events, including five majors. She had also captured eleven doubles titles—playing with Venus—two mixed doubles championships, and an Olympic gold medal. Off the court, Williams was piling up the *endorsement* income. In 2001 alone, she earned $16 million as an advertising spokesperson. It was official: Williams was a *phenomenon*. "Serena has earned her place in history," said Margaret Court, an Australian who has also held all four titles at once and won a record twenty-four "Grand Slam" singles titles during her career. All told, she won more than sixty major tournaments.

As 2003 dawned, Williams was the big story in women's tennis—bigger even than Venus, who had been so successful during the previous few years. Serena's powerful serve (which reached 120 miles per hour, faster than all but a few men's deliveries), *relentless* forehand, and superior athletic ability, together with her competitive nature and overwhelming will to win, made her practically unstoppable. Every time she entered a tournament, some of the talk was about who would be finishing second, because they believed Williams would surely win. She was that good.

Even though she had moved ahead of her sister in the world rankings, Williams had hardly left her family behind. Part of her success came from her close bond to Venus and to their parents, Richard and Oracene. The Williams sisters had to endure jealousy from competitors, racial slurs from other players' fans, and the envy that arose when Serena and Venus began to lead. They did the hard work and overcame the obstacles, but they earned the rewards. And when African-American girls began picking up tennis rackets and tried to copy Serena and Venus's success, they could be happy that they had inspired a whole new generation of champions.

Serena runs her way to yet another win!

It always came back to family. When Serena won in Australia, she was upset for Venus. As the best players in the world—Venus was ranked second as Serena rolled to her "Slam"—the sisters often played each other in *tourney* finals. Neither liked it, but they played on. And when it was over, they went back to being inseparable best friends. Serena and Venus against the world.

New puppy tucked under her arm, Williams heads off to celebrate her win in the singles championship, and her win with her sister, Venus, in the doubles championship, at the 1999 U.S. Open.

"For us, family is number one," Serena said. "People come and go, and friends come and go, but your family has to be there. That's why Venus and I get along so well. We play each other in the finals, and in the end, for me, it's 'OK, after this match, I'm still going to be her sister.' Ten years from now, it's not going to matter who won."

Richard and Oracene taught their daughters to be more than just tennis stars. They *instilled* a strong sense of family in Serena and Venus. And they encouraged them to be well-rounded. That's why Serena has so many different interests. She speaks French and is teaching herself Portuguese. She attends classes at the Art Institute of Miami and hopes to be a fashion designer one day. She has taken acting lessons and has appeared on television shows and music videos.

Serena is a lively young woman, interested in the same things a college senior might be. She loves watching *SpongeBob SquarePants* on television. She speaks on her cellular

> "People come and go, and friends come and go, but your family has to be there. That's why Venus and I get along so well. We play each other in the finals, and in the end, for me, it's 'OK, after this match, I'm still going to be her sister.' Ten years from now, it's not going to matter who won."
>
> —Serena Williams

phone for hours a day. She plays with her two dogs. She can shop forever. She spends hours sitting in a mirror-filled bathroom, adjusting makeup, talking to friends, and dreaming. And just try to keep her from laughing. "If you can't laugh yourself out of a situation, then life gets a bit too stressful, or you just won't be happy," Williams says.

Given Williams's status after her win in Australia, it was hard to imagine that she would be anything less than filled with joy.

Serena gets a hug from her number one fan—her dad, Richard Williams.

CHAPTER TWO

The Dream Begins

It was every parent's nightmare. Venus and Serena were playing tennis on courts in the rough Los Angeles suburb of Compton in 1986 when a car drove by. A local gang member was standing inside, with his head and torso sticking out of the sunroof.

He was holding a gun.

He fired on the courts, again and again. Venus and Serena ran to safety. So did Richard, who was there with them. No one was hurt, but it was clear that somebody did not like the idea of the Williams sisters working on their games. When the girls got home, they told Oracene, who was furious. But not scared. She understood that being *ambitious* when you lived in a tough neighborhood meant being strong. The girls kept playing at the courts and never experienced another incident like that one. Pretty soon, they would be out of Compton and free of its dangers.

"If you acted like a chump [there], they treated you like one," Oracene said.

Richard Williams had moved his family to Compton in April 1983, to build his business of offering low-cost health insurance to poorer families. Serena, who was born on

September 26, 1981, in Saginaw, Michigan, wasn't even two years old. She was the youngest of five girls—three half-sisters, Yetunde, Isha, and Lyndrea—with whom she shared a mother. She and Venus had the same mother and father. All five were raised as full sisters. Tragically, Yetunde was shot and killed at age thirty-one in September 2003, in Compton, California. Serena, like the whole family and the nation, grieved.

Life was easier when she was a child. Like many little sisters, Serena looked up to her older siblings, particularly Venus, who had been born nearly two years earlier. When the family went out to dinner, Serena would order what Venus did. She played with Venus's toys, even when she was not supposed to.

"I liked being the baby. I could cry and whine as much as I wanted until I got my way. All of my sisters spoiled me," Serena said.

"She used to be terrible," Venus said.

In 1986, not long after Venus had picked up a racket, Serena did the same. Many have heard the story of how Richard directed his children into tennis. He was sitting in his house, watching a women's tournament on television one day, when he saw the winner—Virginia Ruzici—accept a check for $30,000. All that, just for knocking a ball over a net. That settled it. Venus and Serena would play tennis.

So Richard studied books and videotapes to learn the game. He would take the children to hit day after day, ball after ball. Soon, the girls started to play in junior tournaments throughout Southern California. Venus excelled, and Serena showed she had talent, too. One day when she was eight, Serena entered herself in a tournament in Indian Wells, California. She filled out all the forms herself, without telling her parents. She advanced to the final, where she met—and lost to—

> **"I liked being the baby. I could cry and whine as much as I wanted until I got my way. All of my sisters spoiled me."**
> **—Serena Williams**

Venus. It was the first time the sisters would meet in a tourney. It would not be the last.

When Serena was nine, she and Venus accepted scholarships to the Rick Macci Tennis Academy in Florida. The decision to enter the exclusive training center wasn't considered a severe change from the accepted training customs of the time. But when Richard decided to withdraw each girl from junior competition, many in the tennis community thought he was crazy. How would the girls develop away from strong *opposition*? Keeping them in a family-dominated *cocoon* could only damage their development. Or could it?

"That was a great plan," says Dave Rineberg, who spent seven years (1992–1999) as a hitting coach with the Williams sisters. "He let them have a pretty normal childhood. They weren't burning out."

Richard was thinking about his children as more than just tennis players. He wanted them to grow in many directions, to have several interests. That's why he encouraged them to try as many different subjects as they could in school. That is also why he would pull them off the courts for weeks at a time to take them on vacations. He had seen what happened to players who did nothing but whack the fuzzy ball. Richard had learned his lessons well. As a child, he worked in cotton fields to earn money. He had to drop out of high school at age sixteen to make money for his family. He did not want his children to have to do that.

"There's a method to my madness," he said. "The goals were for my girls to be good people and also to be the most powerful tennis players out there."

> **"That was a great plan. He let them have a pretty normal childhood. They weren't burning out."**
> **—Dave Rineberg**

Richard let Rick Macci and Dave Rineberg handle the finer points of tennis. He would take care of everything else. Since 1989, he had been receiving advice about how to direct the girls' careers from Keven Davis, a Seattle-based sports agent. Few knew that. Many in

Richard and Serena watch Venus Williams play in the 2000 U.S. Open finals in New York.

junior tennis circles thought Richard was acting alone. And acting poorly. They didn't realize he was consulting others before taking action. Richard wanted to be the one people criticized. He wanted his daughters to be left alone. He used his experience as a businessman and what he learned from his own childhood to teach them to be tough. He wanted them to be prepared for everything that would happen off the court, too.

"I taught them how to handle problems and solve them, to walk through them and not around them," Richard said. "I told them that's what rich people do. You can't wait for a situation to happen to get ready for it."

But for all Richard's training, there was no way—none at all—he could have prepared his girls for what happened when they became professional players.

> "There's a method to my madness. The goals were for my girls to be good people and also to be the most powerful tennis players out there."
> —Richard Williams

Only sixteen, Serena (left) prepares for her debut—at the Direct Line Ladies Tennis Championships in England. Her sister Venus is there along with her.

CHAPTER THREE

First Steps

It was not a debut that drew much fanfare. In fact, when Serena finally began playing professionally, in October 1995, nobody really noticed. The site was Quebec City, Canada, which was about as removed from the bright lights of women's professional tennis as could be. It was not even a tournament, but a qualifier for an event. And Williams lost, 6-1, 6-1.

After that, the fourteen-year-old Williams stopped playing professional tennis for more than a year.

While Venus was beginning her climb to the top, Serena waited. She was in no hurry, and neither was Richard. Just as he had kept his daughters off the junior circuit when they were younger, so too would he make sure Serena was not rushed into anything. She was still the baby.

So, 1996 was a year to hit the ball with coaches and learn the game. And grow. She did not travel, except to watch Venus play. Meanwhile, she had plenty of schoolwork. True to his goal, Richard was making sure his youngest daughter would have as "normal" a childhood as possible.

That changed in 1997—in grand style. Serena joined the tour, and after failing to qualify for tournaments in Indian Hills and Los Angeles, California, and Zurich, Switzerland, she earned a place in a tournament in Moscow, Russia. She lost quickly there but made headlines in November, at a tournament in Chicago, by upsetting Mary Pierce, then ranked number seven in the world, in the second round, and fourth-ranked Monica Seles in the quarterfinals. Though Serena lost to Lindsay Davenport in the semifinals, she had made it clear that she could play the game. The world's 304th-ranked player had knocked off two of the game's giants, making her the lowest-ranked player ever in tour history to defeat two top-10 players in the same tournament. Her win over Seles made her the lowest-ranked player in seven years to knock off a top-5 rival.

Serena may have been shorter than Venus (by about four inches, or ten centimeters), but she had the same determination and power as her sister. And now, it looked like she would have the same success. Former tour standout Pam Shriver certainly thought so. In the mid-1990s, she spent time training with Serena and Venus and came away impressed. "Serena's forehand wasn't that big on control, but as far as power . . . Wow!" Shriver said. "She was just cracking the ball."

Yes, Serena still had a lot to learn, but she had talent. That much was clear. She had tremendous speed and quickness. She got to just about everything on the court. And, as Shriver said, she could pound the ball.

"She hit some great shots," Seles said after losing to Serena in Chicago. "You have to *attribute* that to her being a great athlete."

Williams had something else going for her—she was fierce. That set her apart from Venus, who was much more controlled on the court and less interested in *demoralizing* her opponents. Like her idol, former men's great John McEnroe, Serena brought an *intensity* to her play. After her success in Chicago, Serena said that she wanted to win every point she played. That attitude—at least outwardly—was different from Venus's approach. During a *changeover* between games during one of her 1997 U.S. Open matches, Venus had a much-publicized run-in with Irina Spirlea, during which Spirlea wouldn't move to one side, as the two players walked toward each other. When asked how Serena would have handled that, Richard Williams issued something of a warning.

"[Spirlea] ought to be glad it wasn't Serena she bumped into," he said. "She would have been decked."

He wasn't kidding. But Williams was easygoing off the court. She enjoyed every minute of life, whether it was shopping for sunglasses before heading to scorching hot Australia for the 1998 Australian Open or hanging out with Venus between matches. She delighted in rating the male players on the tour according to their looks, placing Pete Sampras at

> "Serena's forehand wasn't that big on control, but as far as power . . . Wow! She was just cracking the ball."
> —Pam Shriver

How to Keep Score in Tennis

The system by which scores are kept in tennis games may seem confusing, but it is quite logical—once you get the hang of it.

The object of the game is to win the match. To do that, a player must win a majority of the sets played. For instance, some matches are best-of-three sets. That means the first one to take two sets is the winner. All professional women's and most men's indoor matches are best-of-threes. Outdoors, women still play best-of-three, while men often play best-of-five. A player must capture three sets to win one of those.

A set consists of games. To win a game, a player must take at least four points. But games aren't scored 0-1-2-3-4. Zero in tennis is known as "love." The first point is 15, so a player who leads 1-0 actually is ahead 15-0. The next point is scored 30, then 40. One more point gives a player the game. The twist is that a game must be won by two points. So, someone leading 40-30 who gets a point wins a game. But if a game is tied, 40-40, the next point does not win. In fact, tennis has a name for a tie like that—"deuce." The next point won gives the player an "advantage." If the advantage goes to the server, it's called "ad in." If the other player gets the point, it's "ad out." A player who wins a point while holding advantage wins the game. If the opponent does, it's back to deuce. So, when two players reach deuce, one of them must win two straight points to capture a game.

It takes six games to win a set. But again, you must win by two games. If a player leads 5 games to 4, and then loses the next game, making it 5-5, the set extends to seven games. But if there is a 6-6 tie, players use a "tiebreaker." In that case, the first player to earn five points wins—by two. The winner of a tiebreaker takes the set, 7-6. There are a few exceptions. At Wimbledon, the last set of a match doesn't end in a tiebreaker. Instead, players continue until someone wins by two games, even if the score is 16-14!

A fierce competitor, Serena hits a backhand to Irina Spirlea in the 1998 Australian Open. Williams won the match, 6-7.

the top of the list. But she also wanted to win, and she worked hard to accomplish that goal.

"With Venus, everything comes so easy," Oracene said. "It's just a natural ability, no matter what it is, athletic or academic. With Serena, it comes a little bit harder, but it makes her work harder, too. She's more of a stick-to-it person."

Serena was not yet ready to blossom, but she had proven that her future was bright. As she discovered in the coming years, she would have to be patient. No matter who else she beat on the tour, there was still one person who would be ahead of her: Venus.

It wasn't a straight line to the top. Serena Williams hangs her head after losing a point in a match against Martina Hingis at the Lipton Tennis Championships in 1998.

CHAPTER FOUR

Venus's Little Sister

Defeat is never fun. Losing hurts, and Williams felt bad when she lost to Martina Hingis in the quarterfinals of the 1998 Lipton Championships in Key Biscayne, Florida. Williams was moving slowly up the women's tennis ladder, winning just enough to keep her name on people's lips but never taking the next step by winning important tournaments. Yes, she had reached the semifinals of the Adidas International, in Australia. But Serena had not yet arrived.

Venus, on the other hand, was there. And after Serena lost to Hingis, she did what she always did—went right to her sister. Serena needed a shoulder to cry on, but she had something to offer in return—a tip for beating Hingis.

"Serena gave me one pointer that really helped me," Venus said after she had defeated Hingis in the semifinals, 6-2, 5-7, 6-2. "I will not disclose [it] to y'all for fear that it will appear in the papers and all over television."

Team Williams was moving along quite nicely in 1998. Serena beat some top-flight players. Her performance in Australia included a win over third-ranked Lindsay Davenport. But she was young and *inconsistent*. Venus, meanwhile, had climbed into the top 10 and was on the edge of true stardom. Her run to the U.S. Open finals the

Williams is so intent on her game she looks as though she is in pain!

previous September was evidence of that. She was the main Williams sister and had proved it at the Australian Open when she defeated Serena, 7-6, 6-1, in the second round. It was the first time the sisters had met in professional competition. They each played ferociously. But Big Sister won.

Not that there was much joy in the triumph. A battle of the two Williams women was never a happy occasion. Sure, it meant that they were moving closer to taking over the tennis world, as Richard had predicted they would. But it also meant they would have to put away their friendship and love and compete against each other. That wasn't easy.

"I always want Serena to win," Venus said. "I'm the big sister. I take care of Serena. I make sure she has everything, even if I don't have anything."

That was true, as hard as it was for some to understand. Richard's family-first preaching had stuck. Serena and Venus would not become rivals in the bitter, win-at-all-costs sense. Each wanted to win, but never at the expense of the other.

"If dreams came true, Serena and I would be number one in doubles and numbers one and two in singles," Venus said.

It would be awhile before that could happen. Not that the sisters were not making progress. As Venus enjoyed a successful 1998, Serena continued to announce herself as a force on the tour. She reached the quarterfinals of the Italian Open, defeating two top-20 players along the way. Of course, she lost to Venus in that quarterfinal match. Serena made it to the fourth round of the French Open and held a 6-4, 5-2 lead over eventual-champion Arantxa Sanchez-Vicario, before losing. She was more successful on the doubles circuit, winning two championships with Venus and capturing the mixed doubles titles (with Max Mirnyi of Belarus) at Wimbledon and the U.S. Open. By season's end, Serena had earned $2.6 million in prize money and was ranked in the top 20. She was attracting attention.

"Serena is a ferocious competitor and has the fire and the strength," said former tennis great Billie Jean King. "But in addition to her athletic skills, she's a great entertainer. She has a warm personality, and she loves the audience."

Williams made news off the court in 1998, too. In January, she signed a $12 million endorsement contract with Puma, which manufactures sports clothing and equipment. That August, she graduated from the Driftwood Academy, a private preparatory school in Florida, with a 3.0 grade point average.

As impressive as all of that was, 1999 would be even better for Williams. She won five singles titles and finished the year ranked fourth in the world—in only her third full season. Her first-ever singles title came at the Paris Indoor Championships and was accomplished the same day that Venus won a title in Oklahoma City, Oklahoma.

In late March, the sisters met for the first time in a final, at the Lipton Championships.

Victory is sweet! Williams kisses the Evert Cup after winning her match against Steffi Graf.

▼ Althea Gibson

In baseball, Jackie Robinson broke the color barrier. For women's tennis, it was Althea Gibson. The long right-hander with the quick feet and aggressive game won five major titles and helped inspire many young African-American players.

Born in 1927, in Silver, South Carolina, Gibson moved to New York at age three with her family. In 1941, at age fourteen, she began taking tennis lessons. One year later, she entered and won her first tournament, which was sponsored by the all-black American Tennis Association (ATA). In 1947, she embarked on a winning stretch, in which she would earn ten straight ATA championships.

After capturing the 1950 ATA title, Gibson entered the U.S. National Tennis Championships—the *precursor* to the U.S. Open—becoming the first African American to do so. She took her first match but was defeated in the second round. By 1956, there was no stopping Gibson. She won the French championships—her first major—and enjoyed success on the Australian circuit. The following year, Gibson reigned supreme at both Wimbledon and the U.S. championships. In 1958, she did it again—and then retired from amateur tennis. (There was no professional women's tour yet.) In 1960, Gibson toured with basketball barnstormers, the Harlem Globetrotters, playing *exhibition* tennis matches before the Globetrotters' games and at halftime. Four years later, she took up golf and played on the Ladies Professional Golf Association tour. In 1971, she turned professional, but her advanced age made it hard for her to compete against younger, stronger players. That could not erase her previous accomplishments or lessen her impact on the American sporting scene. Althea Gibson died on September 29, 2003, at age seventy-six.

Althea Gibbons broke the color barrier in tennis in the 1950s as the first African American to win Wimbledon and the U.S. national title.

It was the first such sisters match since Maud Watson beat her sister, Lillian, to win at Wimbledon in 1884. And the match went to Venus, 6-1, 4-6, 6-4. It was a hard-fought battle, and afterward, Venus could see the future.

"The way we're both playing, it was inevitable we'd meet in a final," she said. "And it's inevitable we'll meet again."

> **"I always want Serena to win. I'm the big sister. I take care of Serena. I make sure she has everything, even if I don't have anything."**
>
> **—Venus Williams**

That may have been certain, but nobody could have predicted what would happen at the 1999 U.S. Open. *Seeded* seventh, Serena charged through the field, defeating fourth-ranked Monica Seles in the quarters, second-ranked Lindsay Davenport in the semifinals, and top-rated Martina Hingis in the final to win the first Williams family major singles title. It was an enormous breakthrough for Serena, who became the first African-American woman to win a major championship (Australian, French, and U.S. Opens, and Wimbledon) since Althea Gibson did it in 1958.

Winning [the Open] was really like a dream come true," she said. "When that ball *sailed long* on match point, I was just really overwhelmed with emotion. I didn't know whether to laugh or cry, so I did both."

Serena achieved another milestone just a month later, defeating Venus for the first time, in the finals of the Grand Slam Cup. She was no longer the "little sister," but one of the best tennis players in the world. Serena would never surrender her bond with her sister, but on the court she had become her own player.

And what a player she was.

Yes! Williams screams at match point as she defeats Martina Hingis at the 1999 U.S. Open.

CHAPTER FIVE

Still Searching

The 1999 U.S. Open had been a big step for Serena. She was now the Williams sister on everybody's minds, the one about whom everybody spoke. But it was not the best tournament for the family. Richard had predicted years before that Serena would be the better player. Many had *scoffed* at his prediction. But he was looking pretty smart after the Open.

Oracene, meanwhile, was not so pleased. Things had not worked out according to her plan. Venus was the oldest, so, according to Oracene, she was supposed to win the first major tournament. That would have been right. It was the natural way for things to happen. While happy for Serena, she was hurt for Venus, as any mother would be.

"She thinks [that] since she's the oldest, she should've been the first, that maybe she should have been tougher," Oracene said. "That's something they've thought about all their lives: meeting in a final, two sisters. [Venus] feels she let everybody down."

Venus and Serena didn't disappoint CBS, the television network that carried the 1999 Open. Ratings for their match improved an astounding 100 percent over the previous year's final. That statistic did not escape Serena, who understood that she had helped rekindle the nation's interest in women's tennis. Her game, her personality, and even the electric yellow tennis dress she wore during the tourney were perfect for the bright lights.

Always intense, Williams concentrates on the ball as she prepares to serve.

"I touch everyone," she said after defeating Martina Hingis. "Everyone wants to see me. I don't blame them: got to get a look at Serena."

The rest of the tennis community was watching, too. And it was impressed. André Agassi, who won the 1999 Open men's *draw*, came away from the tournament an even bigger Serena fan than before. Like just about everyone else, he chose to compare Serena to Venus, rather than to any other member of the women's tour. It was natural. Although there were still strong players out there, such as Hingis, Lindsay Davenport, and Jennifer Capriati, the Williams sisters were the new generation. And for now, Serena was The One.

"I like her game," Agassi said of Serena. "She and Venus are incredible athletes, but it's my belief that Serena was more ready to win a big tournament. Her second serve is a lot better. Her forehand is better. And she's a more efficient mover."

After beating Venus at the Grand Slam Cup later that year, Serena headed into 2000 on quite a roll. She was ranked fourth in the world and appeared ready to charge to the top of the charts. But 2000 wasn't to be the golden year so many expected. Serena's game didn't let her down; her body did. Injuries bothered her throughout the season. First, it was a *ligament* in her right knee. Next, a small bone in her left foot became inflamed. Then, she tore the *meniscus* in her left knee. So much for the first half of the season. Although Serena won three tournaments—in Los Angeles; Hanover, Germany; and Tokyo—she wasn't the same successful player who had torn through the last part of 1999.

Once again winners, the Williams sisters show off their gold Olympic medals in women's doubles tennis in 2000.

Then came Wimbledon, and the old Serena was back. She charged through the first five rounds of play, surrendering just thirteen games in the process. That was the fewest anyone had dropped during that stretch at Wimbledon since Chris Evert lost only ten in 1976. Waiting for her in the semifinals was Venus, who had endured injury problems of her own throughout the first half of the year. This time, Big Sister prevailed and

Giants of Women's Tennis

The Williams sisters have enjoyed tremendous success during their relatively short careers, but they need to do a lot more before they can top some of the giants of women's tennis.

One of the first to dominate the scene was Brazil's Maria Bueno, who won three Wimbledon crowns and four U.S. Open titles from 1959 to 1966. Even more impressive are the accomplishments of Margaret Court, an Australian who holds the record with twenty-four major singles titles. Court also captured nineteen doubles and nineteen mixed doubles major crowns. In 1970, she won the Grand Slam, taking all four majors in a single year.

American Billie Jean King never won a Grand Slam, but she did take twelve major singles championships, sixteen doubles crowns, and eleven mixed doubles titles. In 1972, she captured the French Open, Wimbledon, and U.S. Open tournaments.

Perhaps the greatest American women's tennis player of all time is Chris Evert, who won eighteen major singles crowns and three doubles titles. Evert never held all four titles at the same time, but from 1974 to 1986 she was quite a force, winning seven French Open titles and five U.S. Open crowns.

German Steffi Graf is second with twenty-two major titles. From the late 1980s through the late 1990s, she was clearly the world's best. In 1988, she won the Grand Slam, and in three other years held three of the four titles.

For endurance, mixed with tremendous achievement, no one can touch Martina Navratilova, who was born in the Czech Republic but became a U.S. citizen in the 1980s. Navratilova has won eighteen major singles crowns, thirty-one doubles titles, and eight mixed doubles crowns. At the 2003 Australian Open, at the age of forty-six, she became the oldest woman to win a tour championship when she captured the mixed doubles title.

Tennis great Billie Jean King (left) and Serena Williams applaud and yell from the stands as Venus Williams receives the Olympic gold medal in women's singles in 2000.

went on to win the tournament. It would be the beginning of a great two-year run for Venus, who would win Wimbledon and the U.S. Open in both 2000 and 2001. But Serena wasn't without her triumphs. She teamed with Venus to win the Wimbledon doubles title and then joined her sister on the victory stand at the 2000 Olympics as doubles champions. As 2000 closed, Serena was still among the world's top-10 players.

She and Venus were also having an effect on the African-American community. Years before, tennis stars Althea Gibson and Arthur Ashe had inspired young African Americans to pick up tennis rackets and head to the courts. Now, the Williams sisters were doing the same thing. All over the country, new faces were appearing at youth clinics and tournaments. That wasn't all. When Serena showed up to play a World Team Tennis match in Delaware, half of the assembled crowd of 2,200 was African American. In Compton, California, African-American children were heading out to the same courts on which Richard had taught Serena and Venus to play the game. One even told an instructor he considered the court "hallowed [sacred] ground." Like Tiger Woods, who had inspired young African Americans to start playing golf, Venus and Serena were role models for a new generation of tennis players.

"Oh, yeah, big time," said Bernard Chavis, president of the American Tennis Association, which has a membership that is almost completely African American. "We're seeing black kids

> "We're seeing black kids picking up racquets for the first time like never before. I can't put a number on it, but I definitely see a Tiger Woods effect. "
>
> —Bernard Chavis

Here, Williams looks almost at ease as she hits a return against Barbara Rittner during a 2001 Wimbledon match. Williams won, 6-4, 6-0.

picking up racquets for the first time like never before. I can't put a number on it, but I definitely see a Tiger Woods effect. It started when Serena won the [U.S.] Open, and it [has gone] way up [since] Venus won Wimbledon."

If African Americans needed more inspiration to play tennis, they would get it in the coming years, as Serena would roar to the top of the tennis world. First, though, she had to do a little soul-searching and commit to being a champion.

Her whole body is stretched as Williams returns a backhand to Madagascar's Dally Randriantefy during the 2002 French Open.

CHAPTER SIX

On Top of the World

The turning point came—of all times—during a long, dull plane ride, after she had to drop out of a match. The 2001 season had not been bad for Serena. She had won three titles, reached the U.S. Open finals (before losing to Venus), and finished the year in the top 10 for the third straight season. For 99 percent of the tennis world, that would have been a great season.

For Serena, it was ordinary. And the Williams sisters were not raised to be ordinary. She was not jealous of Venus's success; the sisters were too close for that. Instead, Serena had become upset with herself. Injuries continued to limit her effectiveness, but just about every player battled some physical trouble.

Serena felt she was hurting herself in other ways. She thought she was not focusing on her game as closely as she should have, but devoting too much time to outside interests. She was taking design classes at the Art Institute of Fort Lauderdale in Florida. Companies were approaching her to endorse their products—and she was accepting. Serena indulged her love of the spotlight with acting lessons. She loved to shop. She loved to stay in constant contact with her friends. She was living the fun life of a successful young adult, and it was costing her on the court.

At the 2001 Australian Open, she committed 36 *unforced errors*, en route to a 6-2, 6-4 loss, her fifth straight to Venus. When she arrived in Sydney for the 2002 Open, Serena was determined to win again, to capture her first major title in more than two years. But she sprained her ankle in a tune-up tournament and had to withdraw from the Australian Open. So much for the dramatic return to prominence. And so much for not paying attention to her sport. On the flight home, Serena made a commitment to tennis. She would concentrate on her training and get back to the top.

As Serena put it later in the year, it would require a better "overall focus—working harder, being more dedicated to tennis and not other things. I didn't have as many distractions in my life. I made a very big commitment to go all out."

The first step came in late March, at the Nasdaq-100 Open tournament. Serena met Venus in the semifinals and pounded her way to a 6-2, 6-2 win. It was all there, the white-hot serve, the big, bad groundstrokes. Serena had announced her return the best way she could, by beating Venus.

"This was the biggest win of my career," Serena said after the match. "This definitely is a milestone for me and all the younger sisters and brothers out there. I was just playing unbelievable. It definitely removed a mental block for me."

Serena whipped Jennifer Capriati in the final, overcoming seven match points in the process. By winning the tourney, she became the second player in history (Steffi Graf was the other) to defeat the world's top-3 players (Capriati, Venus, and Hingis) in the same tournament. But Serena was not finished. No way. She went to Paris and won the French Open in grand style, coming back from a 3-6, 5-6 deficit to stun Capriati in the semifinals and then defeat Venus in the final. The win vaulted her to second in the world rankings, behind Venus. But that was not enough. Serena had a goal, and she was going after it.

"When I'm playing decent tennis, it's really hard for anyone to beat me," Serena said. "I was serious in the beginning of the year when I said [I was going to be number one].

Venus (left) and Serena Williams hug after the 2002 U.S. Open. Serena defeated Venus, 6-4, 6-3.

That's where I want to be, the top spot. If I can't do it, then I won't be giving any more interviews, because I won't be on the tour anymore."

To many, that sounded like the same *bluster* that had come from Richard, back when he was declaring to all who would listen that his girls would be the biggest thing to hit tennis. While Serena's flair for the dramatic did influence her at times, she was serious about reaching the top. The rest of 2002 proved that. Serena went to Wimbledon and won it without losing a set. She and Venus squared off in the first all-sister final at the tournament since 1884. The sisters then teamed up to win the doubles crown, their fifth Grand Slam title together. Although knee problems caused Serena to lay low for part of the ensuing summer tour, she was back at full strength in September for the U.S. Open and had big plans.

And again! Serena backhands to her sister during the women's final of the 2002 French Open Tennis tournament.

"When I'm playing decent tennis, it's really hard for anyone to beat me. I was serious in the beginning of the year when I said [I was going to be number one]. That's where I want to be, the top spot. If I can't do it, then I won't be giving any more interviews, because I won't be on the tour anymore."

—Serena Williams

Williams does not like to miss. Here, she seems about to hit her head with her racquet after missing a shot in the Toyota Princess tennis tournament on September 21, 2002.

Serena arrived in New York ready to play and ready to thrill. She wore a skintight catsuit in some matches, delighting the fans and sending photographers into over-drive. Her play was equally eye-popping. Serena charged to the finals, with a small second-set lapse (she trailed at one point, 5-2, before winning in straight sets) against Lindsay Davenport in the semifinals, the only bump in her road. She then bumped off Venus to win the title and rose to the top spot in the world rankings. It was another *virtuoso* perform-ance by the Williams sisters.

"It's the most amazing thing in sports, almost," Davenport said.

"Could you imagine Tiger Woods challenging a sibling to go head-to-head for all the majors? And in an individual sport. They don't even have teammates to help them along."

But they have each other. Serena's three 2002 major titles and her 2003 Australian Open win gave her the "Serena Slam." Her 2002 performance earned her nearly $4 million in prize money, the most ever earned by a female tennis player. She was on top of the tennis world, making good on her promise. And right behind her, ranked second, was Venus. It was Serena's time at the top, but it was the Williams's world.

And it was growing more wonderful with every swing of the racket.

Serena celebrates her win at the Australian Open tournament in 2003.

Born: September 26, 1981
Height: 5' 10" (1.8 m)
Weight: 145 lbs. (65 kg)
Plays: Righthanded (two-handed backhand)

Grand Slam Titles:

6 (1999 U.S. Open; 2002 French Open, Wimbledon, U.S. Open; 2003 Australian Open, Wimbledon)

Total Titles:

23 singles; 11 doubles; 2 mixed doubles

Won-Loss Record:

246–44 (through September 2003)

Career Earnings:

$12,291,030 (through September 2003)

Year-Ending Rankings:

1997: 99; 1998: 20; 1999: 4; 2000: 6; 2001: 6; 2002: 1

Source: www.wtatour.com

GLOSSARY

ambitious—Interested in accomplishing things and becoming successful.

attribute (verb)—Explain.

bluster—To talk or act in a noisy way and direct others' attention to you.

changeover—The times during a tennis match, occurring after every two games, when players switch sides of the court and resume play after a brief rest.

cocoon—A safe, comfortable place in which a person, usually someone who is young, is able to grow and develop, away from any distractions or dangers.

controversy—A long argument about something between people with great differences of opinion.

demoralizing—Causing someone to lose spirit and hope. In sports, this can be a particularly disappointing loss or ill-timed injury.

dominance—One's ability to control others. In sports, this control refers to a player's or team's continued success.

draw—The path which a person must take in order to win a tennis tournament. This is comprised of each match in which a player must participate as he or she advances further in the competition.

endorsement—A person's support of someone or something. Many athletes make extra money by lending their names to a product that a company is trying to sell.

exhibition—A sporting event which takes place entirely for entertainment and has no bearing on any serious competition.

exuberance—Extra enthusiasm for something or someone.

inconsistent—Uneven in level of performance.

instill(ed)—To put into someone's mind or character over a long period of time.

intensity—The degree or amount of a certain quality or condition. This also refers to the drive with which a person approaches a particular situation.

ligament—A strong band of tissue that connects bones together or holds organs in place inside the body.

meniscus—A curved bit of tissue found inside the knee, which helps keep the bones from grinding against one another.

opposition—The player or team against which someone is playing.

phenomenon—A person, object, or event that is rare and extraordinary. In athletics, this pertains to a new player or team that is unusually successful.

precursor—Something that takes place before something else and usually sets the stage for the second event.

relentless—Constant and never ending.

sailed long—What happens when a tennis ball is hit too hard and travels in the air beyond one of the court's boundaries.

scoff—To look at or speak about someone or something without respect.

seeded—A way of ranking players. Before each competition, organizers determine the order in which they think players will finish. The top seed is expected to have the best chance to win.

tourney—Short for *tournament*. This refers to a competition involving many participants.

unforced errors—A player's mistakes that are deemed to be his or her own fault and not caused by the superior play of an opponent.

virtuoso—A particularly skilled or capable performance that is generally with few flaws.

Find Out More

Books

Gutman, Bill. *Venus & Serena: The Grand Slam Williams Sisters*. New York: Scholastic Paperbacks, 2001.

Hill, Mary. *Serena & Venus Williams* (Real People). Danbury, CT: Children's Press, 2003.

Schimel, Lawrence. *Venus & Serena Williams*. Kansas City, MO: Andrews McMeel Publishing, 2000.

Sparling, Ken, and Joseph Romain (eds.). *Serena and Venus Williams: (Champion Sport Biographies)*. Toronto, Ontario, Canada: Warwick Publishing, 2000.

Web Sites

CBS Sportsline
www.sportsline.com/tennis/players/playerspap/201739

ESPN
http://msn.espn.go.com/tennis/s/wta/profiles/swilliams.hml

INDEX

Page numbers in **boldface** are illustrations.